TERRIFYING T. REX

AND OTHER MIGHTY MEAT EATERS!

PAUL HARRISON

ARCTURUS

TYRANNOSAURUS REX

The most famous species of dinosaur is *Tyrannosaurus rex*. Discovered by Barnum Brown in 1902, this immense meat-eater soon captured the public imagination. But even though we have been studying it for over 100 years, there are still plenty of things we don't know about *T. rex*!

Was it king?

Until recently, *Tyrannosaurus rex* was undisputed king of the dinosaurs. It was thought to have been bigger and meaner than any other. But in the 1990s two discoveries threatened to topple this monarch. *Carcharodontosaurus* and *Giganotosaurus* might have been bigger than *T. rex*!

Little arms

Paleontologists have long been puzzled by *T. rex*'s tiny front arms. These forelimbs would not have reached the dinosaur's mouth and the two claws at the end would have been useless for gripping. They must have been there for a reason—we just don't know what it was.

The banana bites back

The mouth of *Tyrannosaurus rex* was filled with over 60 razor-sharp teeth. They were as long as bananas and curved, so that they bent backward into the dinosaur's mouth. This meant that when *T. rex* bit into its prey it was even harder for the unfortunate creature to escape.

T. rex was heavier than an elephant and longer than two minivans parked end to end.

Fact File

How to say it tie-RAN-oh-SORE-us REX
Meaning of name Tyrant lizard king
Family Tyrannosaur
Period Late Cretaceous
Where found North America
Height 13 feet (4 meters)
Length 46 feet (14 meters)
Weight 7.7 tons (7,000 kilograms)
Food Meat
Special features Large, sharp teeth and powerful jaws

TRIASSIC   JURASSIC   CRETACEOUS

ALBERTOSAURUS

When the first *Albertosaurus* was discovered in Alberta, Canada, paleontologists had no idea how interesting and controversial this relative of the *Tyrannosaurus rex* would prove to be.

Close family

Most paleontologists believe that large meat-eating dinosaurs lived and hunted alone. However, *Albertosaurus* might have been the exception to the rule. The remains of nine *Albertosaurus* have been found together. What's more, the dinosaurs appear to be of different ages. This means that the other tyrannosaurs might also live in family groups, but we just haven't found any evidence of this yet.

Mistaken identity

A paleontologist's job is never easy: there's now debate about exactly how many *Albertosaurus* have been found. Some albertosaurs may actually be from another branch of the tyrannosaur family called *Gorgosaurus*. This proves that the tyrannosaur family was a big one with a strong family resemblance—powerful legs, short arms, a big head, and scary teeth.

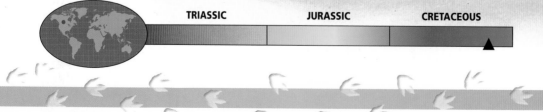

TRIASSIC   JURASSIC   CRETACEOUS

The smallest
Albertosaurus
remains ever found
were those of a
juvenile less than a
quarter the size of
an adult.

Fact File

How to say it al-BERT-o-SORE-us
Meaning of name Alberta lizard
Family Tyrannosauridae
Period Late Cretaceous
Where found North America
Height 11 feet (3.4 meters)
Length 30 feet (9 meters)
Weight 2.8 tons (2,500 kilograms)
Food Meat
Special features Pack hunter

CARCHARODONTOSAURUS

In North Africa, there was a predator that was definitely at the top of the food chain. With a head as big as a person, and a mouth filled with teeth 8 inches (20 centimeters) long, when *Carcharodontosaurus* took a bite, it was a big one!

Biggest ever?

Recent discoveries of *Carcharodontosaurus* have opened up an interesting debate—was this the biggest predator ever? Was it really bigger than *Tyrannosaurus rex*? The evidence seems to suggest it was actually longer, but it also looks as if it had a slighter build. So, taller but lighter? The debate rages on...

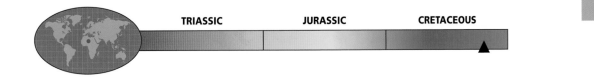

Pack of trouble

A lone *Carcharodontosaurus* was tough enough to take on practically any creature it came across—even some sauropods. It was big, muscular, and fast. However, *Carcharodontosaurus* was also related to *Allosaurus*, so it's possible that this gigantic hunter traveled around in packs. If so, there can't have been a dinosaur alive that felt safe when a group of *Carcharodontosaurus* was on the move.

Fact File

How to say it
kar-KAR-oh-don-toh-SORE-us
Meaning of name Carcharodon lizard
Family Carcharodontosauridae
Period Late Cretaceous
Where found North Africa
Height 12 feet (3.6 meters)
Length 50 feet (15 meters)
Weight 7 tons (6,350 kilograms)
Food Meat
Special features Biggest carnivore of all?

The skull of a Carcharodontosaurus discovered in Morocco in 1996 measured 5 feet 4 inches (1.6 meters).

CARNOTAURUS

One of the stranger-looking dinosaurs, *Carnotaurus* was discovered in that fertile dino-hunting ground that is Patagonia, Argentina—home to some of the more remarkable dinosaur discoveries.

What it looked like

You can guess from *Carnotaurus*'s name what it looked like and what it liked to eat. *Carn* is for carnivore, a meat-eater, while *taurus* is the zodiac sign represented by a bull. One look at that mouth full of teeth is enough to tell you what *Carnotaurus* ate and the two horns on its head were rather bull-like. What puzzles some paleontologists is that the jaws of *Carnotaurus* seem to have been quite weak, an unusual feature in a meat-eater.

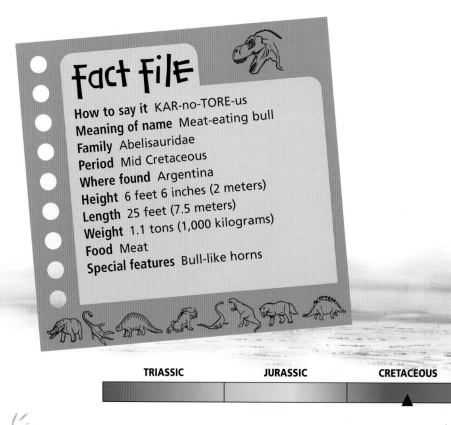

Fact File

How to say it KAR-no-TORE-us
Meaning of name Meat-eating bull
Family Abelisauridae
Period Mid Cretaceous
Where found Argentina
Height 6 feet 6 inches (2 meters)
Length 25 feet (7.5 meters)
Weight 1.1 tons (1,000 kilograms)
Food Meat
Special features Bull-like horns

TRIASSIC   JURASSIC   CRETACEOUS

Stumpy

Although it's a fairly rare dinosaur, we know quite a bit about *Carnotaurus*. It had pebbly skin, rather like a lizard, with bigger bumps near the spine. However, its two arms were very short—even shorter than *Tyrannosaurus rex's*—so paleontologists aren't sure what they were used for.

It's thought that Carnotaurus could get up to quite a speed when it was chasing its prey.

DILOPHOSAURUS

Dilophosaurus was the biggest carnivore of the early Jurassic period. This long-legged meat-eater was probably quite speedy and may have hunted in packs.

Crest and claws

The most striking feature of this amazing predator was its double-crested head, giving it its name. These frills were probably for nothing more than display, but were impressive nonetheless. Another unusual aspect of this dinosaur was its dewclaw—a small claw a little way up the back of each leg—similar to the dewclaws you can see on the legs of domestic dogs and cats.

Weak bite

For a large predator, *Dilophosaurus* had quite a weak bite; paleontologists can tell this from the way the muscles were attached to the jaw. Since it couldn't overpower its prey with one savage bite, *Dilophosaurus* probably slashed with its sharp claws until the victim collapsed from the effects of its injuries.

Fact File

How to say it die-LOF-oh-SORE-us
Meaning of name Two-ridged lizard
Family Coelophysoidae
Period Early Jurassic
Where found USA
Height 5 feet (1.5 meters)
Length 20 feet (6 meters)
Weight 992 pounds (450 kilograms)
Food Meat
Special features Deadly claws

The remains of three Dilophosaurus were found together in Arizona, so it is thought it was a group animal.

TRIASSIC   JURASSIC   CRETACEOUS

HERRERASAURUS

This South American predator was one of the earliest true dinosaurs, roaming the earth nearly 230 million years ago.

Early hunter

Herrerasaurus was a meat-eater, as its sharp teeth clearly indicate, and it used its speed to ambush prey. It also had long, sharp, grasping claws, which were ideal for catching and tearing up meat. *Herrerasaurus* feasted on plant-eating dinosaurs and even on smaller meat-eaters, too.

Hunter or hunted?

Of course, *Herrerasaurus* didn't just eat other dinosaurs, and the dinosaurs didn't have the planet to themselves—other reptiles and insects lived here at the same time. So, although this gave *Herrerasaurus* a wide-ranging menu, it also meant that larger predators might have downed the odd *Herrerasaurus* as a tasty snack themselves.

Herrerasaurus is possibly the oldest of three examples of the earliest meat-eating dinosaurs found in South America.

Fact File

How to say it HAIR-rare-ah-SORE-us
Meaning of name Herrera's lizard
Family Herrerasauridae
Period Early Triassic
Where found Argentina
Height 3 feet 3 inches (1 meter)
Length 10 feet (3 meters)
Weight 165 pounds (75 kilograms)
Food Meat
Special features One of the earliest dinosaurs

TRIASSIC   **JURASSIC**   **CRETACEOUS**

SYNTARSUS

Syntarsus was one of the first meat-eating dinosaurs to have appeared in the Jurassic period. This small dinosaur could run quickly, thanks to its light build. Paleontologists believe that the female *Syntarsus* was larger than the male and a lot more common.

Same but different

Syntarsus was found in both America and Africa, which supports the idea that these two continents were once joined. When they separated, *Syntarsus* began to evolve slightly differently. The American *Syntarsus* grew a pair of small crests on the top of its head—a distinctive feature that was missing from the African species.

One of the gang

Although *Syntarsus* was small and lightly built, it was an effective predator. Much like wolves, *Syntarsus* hunted in packs, so these dinosaurs were very good at tackling much larger animals. However, they were not fussy eaters, and were just as happy feeding on small mammals or scavenging for dead animals.

| TRIASSIC | JURASSIC | CRETACEOUS |

Syntarsus may have had a hopping action, like a kangaroo—useful when escaping predators.

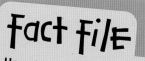

Fact File

How to say it sin-TAR-sus
Meaning of name Fused ankle
Family Ceratosaur
Period Early Jurassic
Where found USA, Africa
Height 2 feet 7 inches (0.8 meter)
Length 10 feet (3 meters)
Weight 51 pounds (23 kilograms)
Food Meat
Special features Fast runner

Picture credits

© Shutterstock: back cover.

© De Agostini Picture Library: title page; pages 4–9; pages 12–15.

© Miles Kelly Publishing Ltd: pages 2–3; 10–11.

This edition published in 2012 by Arcturus Publishing Limited
26/27 Bickels Yard, 151–153 Bermondsey Street,
London SE1 3HA

ISBN: 978-1-84858-671-0
CH002335US
Supplier 15, Date 0312, Print run 1747

Printed in China